CW01149889

Original title:
What Do the Reindeers Do?

Copyright © 2024 Creative Arts Management OÜ
All rights reserved.

Author: Alexander Thornton
ISBN HARDBACK: 978-9916-90-846-4
ISBN PAPERBACK: 978-9916-90-847-1

Majestic Shadows of December

In the moonlight, they prance and play,
Hiding from the snowmen, come what may.
With antlers tall, they strike a pose,
Waiting for laughs from frosty foes.

They twirl and leap on frozen ground,
Dancing to music that's just profound.
Chasing snowflakes like lively sprites,
Sipping cocoa on chilly nights.

Lullabies of the Northern Gale

Singing softly, they jingle and sway,
Sharing secrets in a breezy ballet.
They play hopscotch on icy trails,
Trading their stories while the wind exhales.

With cheeky grins, they dodge and weave,
Crafting snowballs on this frosty eve.
Tickling each other, they can't help but laugh,
Taking turns with the snowman's half.

Emissaries of the Winter Whispers

Beneath the stars, they gather and chat,
Debating who's the cutest—imagine that!
They prank each other with snow and ice,
While trying to keep their coats looking nice.

With candy canes offered as peace treaties,
They munch and giggle, sharing sweet feats.
Whispers in glades of twinkling frost,
The reindeers laugh, never feeling lost.

Adventurers Beneath the Aurora

Sailing on clouds in the northern light,
They race the stars, a magical sight.
With every bounce and frolic in tow,
Inventing new games in the shimmer and glow.

They play tag with the northern star's gleam,
Practicing how to glide, oh what a dream!
With giggles echoing in the crisp night air,
They plot their next stunts, plotting with flair.

The Quiet Dance of Winter's Breath

In the stillness, they prance with glee,
Paws tapping rhythms, wild and free.
Their tiny bells ring, a jolly tune,
As snowflakes swirl beneath the moon.

They plot a scheme to steal some treats,
Munch on cookies when no one peeks.
With giggles muffled under the frost,
They'll sneak away, never truly lost.

Kin of the Arctic Night.

Under the stars, they share a joke,
A giant sled, just for a poke.
With antlers high, they tilt their heads,
And tumble down like giant threads.

They challenge each other to a race,
Pushing each other—who's the fastest face?
Each slip on ice brings more hearty laughs,
As they slide around, dancing like calves.

Dancing with Northern Lights

With every shimmer of green and gold,
They spin and leap, a sight to behold.
Their hooves a-tap on the frozen ground,
A reindeer rave, what joy is found!

They twirl in circles, round and round,
Chasing flickers that dance all around.
A jolly band on a winter's spree,
Who knew reindeer could be so free?

Secrets of the Winter Herd

In cozy pines, they share their lore,
Of flying lessons and winter galore.
With a wink and a nod, they keep it hushed,
Their stories of snowstorms leave all flushed.

They wear their bells as badges of pride,
Hiding from elves, they try to confide.
But when the sun dips low in the sky,
Their laughter echoes, oh my, oh my!

Whispers of the Wondrous Frost

In snowflakes' dance, they prance and play,
With antlers tall, they lead the way.
They tickle the trees with giggles and glee,
While crafting snowmen, wild and free.

With carrots and sweets, they build a feast,
Hiding from elves, they jest like beasts.
They slip on ice, a comical sight,
And frolic 'til dawn, what a cheerful night!

Radiance in the Hushed Hues

Under the glow of the moon so bright,
They challenge each other for fun-filled fights.
Rolling in snow, they make quite the mess,
Dressed up in lights, they strut and impress.

They jingle with joy, in playful parade,
With snickers and snorts, they shimmy and fade.
Chasing their tails, they twirl in delight,
Sharing their tales, oh what a sight!

The Sleighbell Serenade

From rooftop to rooftop, they leap and they bound,
Spreading their laughter, oh what a sound!
With bells that jingle, they sing out of tune,
A raucous choir beneath the moon!

They poke at the snow, craft snowball machines,
Firing away like comical fiends.
With a dash and a dash, they zoom past so fast,
Leaving a trail of giggles that last!

Legends of the North Wind

Chasing the clouds, they race through the sky,
With chuckles and hoots, they appear to fly.
Wearing their socks, mismatched and loud,
Strutting their stuff, they're joyful and proud.

In frosty caverns, they play hide and seek,
With echoes of laughter—it's fun that they seek!
As snowflakes swirl, they dance without care,
In legends of joy, they float through the air!

Under the Northern Lights

In the moonlight, they prance and play,
Reindeer games at the end of the day.
With a jig and a hop, they twist and shout,
Who knew they could dance without a doubt?

Twirling around like they own the scene,
Wearing sweaters in colors so bright and keen.
They sing reindeer songs with a silly tune,
Under the shimmering light of the moon.

A Sleigh in the Snow

The sleigh's gone wild, oh what a sight,
As reindeer take flight with all of their might.
Clanging and banging, they zip through the air,
Spreading holiday cheer everywhere!

With a whoosh and a swoosh, they race down the lane,
Chasing each other, oh what a game!
Laughing together as they tumble and roll,
Who knew reindeer had such a playful soul?

Whispers of the Woodland

In the trees, the whispers are clear,
Reindeer gossip as they gather near.
"Did you see that one with the shiny red nose?"
"He thinks he's a star! Everyone knows!"

They chuckle and giggle, sharing old tales,
Of snowy adventures and funny fails.
With a wink and a nod, they plot their next prank,
In the woodland, laughter flows like a riverbank.

Antlers and Stardust

With antlers so grand, they strut with flair,
Decked in glitter, they're quite the pair.
Spreading magic from their very tips,
While doing a dance that makes everyone skip!

They prance through the stars, all shiny and bright,
Leaving trails of stardust that sparkle at night.
"Catch us if you can!" they joyfully tease,
As they leap over hills with the greatest of ease.

Reflections in Frosted Echoes

Beneath the moon's bright gleam, they prance,
Wearing sweaters, they join the dance.
With jingle bells and playful flair,
They giggle as they toss snow in the air.

In every nook, a reindeer peeks,
Making silly faces, playing hide and seeks.
They sip hot cocoa, topped with cream,
And plot the silliest winter dream.

Emblems of Ethereal Journeys

With noses bright and fluffly tails,
They navigate through frosty trails.
In ski gear, they zoom and slide,
As snowflakes whirl in merry pride.

They gather 'round to swap tall tales,
Of daring feats and snowy fails.
With every laugh, the winter sings,
As they dance on ice with silly springs.

The Gathering of Gentle Spirits

At midnight's charm, they share a feast,
Of gummy worms and candy beast.
They trade bright hats with colors bizarre,
While dreaming of their next escapade star.

They ride on clouds made of candy floss,
Telling jokes that make them toss.
With twinkling eyes and hearty glee,
They celebrate their revelry.

Sonnets of the Northern Breeze

Oh, reindeer pals in fluff and cheer,
Who pull great sleighs, devoid of fear.
But when the night gives way to dawn,
They leap and jokingly yawn and yawn.

With frosted hats and boots of gold,
They venture forth, brave and bold.
Each winter's night, they shine so bright,
Making memories full of delight.

The Heralds of Frost

In the frosty air, they prance with glee,
Chasing snowflakes, as wild as can be.
With a jingle here and a stomp so loud,
They gather the laughter of every crowd.

With antlers like crowns, oh what a sight,
Dancing in circles, under moonlight.
They nibble on branches, not a care in sight,
Making their mischief until it's night.

Antlers in the Snow

Antlers adorned with snowflakes bright,
They twirl and tumble, oh what a sight!
Sliding on ice with a giggle and cheer,
Unruly reindeer, spreading the cheer.

Who needs a sleigh when you've got four legs?
They leap through the drifts, avoiding the pegs.
With a wink and a nod, they guarantee fun,
For the merry adventures have only begun.

Whispering Hooves in the Twilight

In the gentle dusk, their hooves softly tread,
Telling secrets of gifts, as if being led.
With a flick of their tails, they stir up the night,
Whispering the tales of their joyful flight.

Bounding through fields with giggles galore,
They plot silly antics while searching for more.
Racing the shadows, with hearts all aglow,
Creating a ruckus wherever they go.

When Snowflakes Fall on Fur

When the snowflakes fall, they roll in delight,
Belly-flopping down hills, oh what a sight!
With a shiver and shake, they wriggle around,
Giggles erupting from soft snowy ground.

They play hide and seek, in the tall winter trees,
With friends like these, it's all about ease.
In a flurry of joy, they frolic and fly,
Making merry memories under the sky.

The Silent Run of the Hoofed Winds

In the moonlight, they prance, oh so spry,
Dancing shadows beneath the sky.
With a flick of their tails, they begin to tease,
While the owls hoot softly, 'Please, not the freeze!'

They dash through the snow, a comical sight,
Laughter echoing into the night.
With each joyful leap, the snowflakes fly,
Even the grumpy old fox starts to sigh.

Vanguard of the Snowbound Trails

In a line they stride, with antlers all bright,
Heading to places that give quite a fright.
They whisper and giggle, to keep up the cheer,
While the snowman grumbles, 'Oh dear, oh dear!'

Their feet like marshmallows, they bounce and glide,
Over the hills, it's a slippery ride.
With a wink and a nudge, they trip over a log,
The grouchy old cat is left in a fog.

Journey Through the Icy Realms

Through icicles and frost, they zip and zoom,
Leaving behind a funny perfume.
With jingle and jangle, their bells do ring,
Making the squirrels dance and sing.

They navigate mazes of cobweb and dew,
Playing hide and seek, like a child would do.
With a tumble and a roll, they chuckle afloat,
While the penguins watch with a baffled gloat.

Ballet of the Blizzards

In the swirling dance of a winter's fling,
They twirl and they leap, oh what a thing!
With grace and humor, they glide on ice,
A performance to see, if you're feeling nice.

As the blizzard blows in, they spin like dervishes,
Creating snow flurries, their playful wishes.
With leaps of joy, and mischief galore,
The walls of the forest resound with roar!

Serendipity in the Snowdrifts

In the brisk of winter's play,
Reindeer dance the night away.
With antlers high, they prance and twirl,
Chasing snowflakes, giving a whirl.

They huddle close for a snowy snack,
Nibbling pine and watching their back.
But squirrels laugh as they slip and slide,
While reindeer grumble, trying to hide.

When Christmas comes, they take their flight,
Painting stars across the night.
But oh, the mess when they land too fast,
Tangled in tinsel, a holiday blast!

With sleigh bells jingling, they race the moon,
Only to trip on a snowman's broom.
They shake it off with a hearty cheer,
These jolly reindeer, the holiday's dear!

Heartbeats of the Frosted Earth

Reindeer gather for a grand parade,
With silly hats and a charade.
They laugh and leap through the frosty trees,
Making snow angels, if you please!

In the sparkle of the morning light,
They play hide and seek, oh what a sight!
Caught in snowdrifts, giggles abound,
These merry creatures, joy is found.

A game of tag on the icy ground,
But watch your step, don't fall down!
With snowballs flying, hearts full of glee,
They make winter feel so carefree.

As the sun sets, they strike a pose,
Waving to stars with a nose that glows.
With a wink at the night, they dash away,
Leaving magic trails for another day!

The Joy of Jingle Bells

Jingle bells and sleighs abound,
Reindeer prance on frosty ground.
They kick and leap, do silly tricks,
While sneaking snacks, what's in the mix?

With every dash, they laugh and play,
Spreading cheer this festive day.
But ho ho ho, what's that they see?
A snowball fight from Tim and Lee!

They dodge and weave, so spry and quick,
Who knew they'd have such nimble kicks?
In twirls and spins, they find delight,
As snowflakes dance in winter's light.

Antlers Against the Sky

Antlers high, they touch the stars,
Playing tag with Venus and Mars.
They leap and soar, so full of glee,
In a cosmic game of hide and seek!

With a wink and a nod, they take to flight,
Twisting through the chilly night.
Their best friend, the moon, laughs along,
As they break out in gleeful song.

Each reindeer thinks they are the best,
In prancing games, they never rest.
With silly hats and goofy stances,
They prance around in wild dances.

Silent Watchers of the Night

On rooftops high, they gaze and stare,
Watching families without a care.
With twinkling lights, they share a grin,
What a sight, oh let the fun begin!

They whisper secrets as they wait,
For cookies baked on a silver plate.
One steals a bite, oh, what a treat,
While others laugh and stomp their feet.

In the stillness, they make a noise,
With giggles and mischief, oh such joys!
They twirl and spin, they make a fuss,
Whispering tales beneath the bus.

Reindeer Dreams in a Winter Wonderland

In dreams they dash through snow so bright,
With candy canes in silly flight.
They sip hot cocoa, so warm and sweet,
Then dash away from the big fat cheat!

They swirl with snowflakes, twinkling white,
Chasing each other in frosty delight.
With every pounce, they tumble and roll,
Sharing laughter that fills the soul.

As morning breaks, they stretch and yawn,
But in a flash, they're gone by dawn.
Yet deep in dreams, they still will play,
Reindeer fun will never sway.

The Spirit of Christmas in Hoofprints

With bells that jingle, they prance and play,
Dashing through snow in a comical way.
They giggle and leap, doing tricks in the air,
Making snow angels without a single care.

Through woods they will wander, munching on snacks,
Nibbling on berries and orange truck snacks.
With a wink and a nod, they share secret cheer,
Painting the town red as the holidays near.

Dreams on Frostbitten Trails

At dawn, they gather for a breakfast feast,
Sipping hot cocoa, they chatter, at least.
With marshmallow hats and scarves knitted tight,
They plot their adventures for the coming night.

Through the snowflakes, they giggle and glide,
Chasing each other, they take quite a ride.
Racing along as the sun starts to dip,
With a little bit of mischief, they'll take a trip.

Under the Glimmer of Stars

Beneath twinkling lights, they dance in a row,
Spinning around while the cold breezes blow.
With a sprinkle of laughter and a dash of cheer,
They summon the magic that brings holiday cheer.

With snowball fights that leave everyone grinning,
Each playful toss, oh, it's just the beginning.
They tumble and roll, a sight to behold,
In a wintery wonderland, their stories unfold.

Lullabies of the Arctic Night

When evening falls, they gather in close,
Telling tall tales of the ones they love most.
With stars up above, they dream up a scheme,
To ride on the clouds, oh, such a wild dream!

In the Arctic hush, they whisper and sigh,
Wishing on snowflakes that flutter on by.
With giggles and snorts, they drift to their beds,
In cozy little nooks, snuggling their heads.

Tracks of the Celestial Herd

In the snow they leave a trail,
Giggles echo, never pale.
Hooves that dance with frosty cheer,
Marking paths for all to hear.

They prance around the glowing trees,
Whispering secrets with the breeze.
A game of tag beneath the stars,
Counting all the snowy cars.

With silly leaps and playful bounds,
They add joy to wintry grounds.
Laughing loudly, causing rumbles,
While careful not to trip on stumbles.

When they see a snowman grin,
It's time for a snowstorm win!
With a wink and playful snort,
They race to town for gifts to sort.

Nighttime Pilgrims

Underneath the moon's bright glow,
They gather joy, a steady flow.
Wobbly legs and twinkling eyes,
Chasing stars like flying pies.

With every leap, a giggle spills,
In the cold with jolly thrills.
Racing through the chilly air,
Who can soar without a care?

They know each cozy cabin warm,
Gathering tales, a winter charm.
While people sleep, their dreams take flight,
The reindeer giggle through the night.

Sneaking treats from kitchens near,
With a snicker, they disappear.
Nose to nose, they plot and scheme,
Creating magic in a dream.

The Journey of the Frosted Hoof

With a hop and a silly sway,
They bounce along in frosty play.
Frosted hooves leave sparkling signs,
As they trail through winter pines.

Dashing through the icy chill,
Laughing quick, they can't stay still.
A snowball fight! Who can throw?
Frosty fun in winter's glow.

Sleek and shiny, they glide and zoom,
Chasing shadows, filling the room.
Kicking snowflakes like confetti,
Jumping high, they stay quite ready.

When dawn creeps in with rosy light,
They spin and twirl, a blizzy sight.
With cheerful hearts and playful peers,
They celebrate the winter years.

Guardians of the Winter Sky

With antlers tall like mighty trees,
They guard the night, the world at ease.
Dressed in snow like powdered kings,
They chat with clouds and whisper wings.

In winter's breath, they take their stance,
Bouncing 'round in a starry dance.
Glancing down, they spot a fawn,
Sharing jokes until the dawn.

Their laughter echoes, fills the air,
As they prance without a care.
Sledding down from moonlit heights,
Turning chilly skies to bright delights.

With every flip, they spread the cheer,
Bringing joy to all who hear.
Oh, the fun that they bestow,
Guardians of the winter glow.

Travelers of the Cold

They bundle up in scarves so bright,
With mittens on, they leap and slide.
In frosty air, they dance with glee,
These travelers of the cold, you see.

They play tag with snowflakes in the sky,
While reindeer prance and wink an eye.
They sip cocoa, all warm and neat,
With chocolate mustaches, oh what a treat!

In the snowy fields, they play hide and seek,
With antlers at play, so unique.
They giggle and laugh, a winter show,
Under the stars, with a glimmering glow.

With sleigh bells ringing, they dash around,
Creating snowmen, round and round.
So if you see them, don't be shy,
Join in the fun, give it a try!

The Enchanted Herd

In a forest where the snowflakes twirl,
Lives a herd of reindeer in a dizzy whirl.
They munch on treats from the trees' own hands,
And wear tiny bells, with sparkling bands.

They frolic and leap in the icy air,
With glittering noses and fluffy hair.
Each time they giggle, a pinwheel spins,
As they twirl in circles with silly grins.

Magical pranks fill the frosty night,
Like flicking snowballs, oh what a sight!
They dance with shadows of the big, bright moon,
And sing reindeer songs with a merry tune.

So if you wander through winter's realm,
Look for the herd, take the helm.
Prepare for laughter, a swift winter's play,
In the enchanted land where they sway!

Spirit of the Icy Forest

In the heart of the forest, oh so bright,
Danced the reindeer with sheer delight.
They wore little hats and twinkling shoes,
Bringing joy and laughter in the frosty hues.

They prance and shuffle, with giggles that soar,
Chasing their tails near the icy shore.
With snowballs flying, they create a mess,
But oh, the fun — it's nothing less!

Every night they share tales profound,
Of fanciful trips across snowy ground.
Their spirits are cheerful, their hearts so wide,
In the icy forest, their joy cannot hide.

So catch a glimpse in the gathering cold,
Of laughter and magic, a sight to behold.
For in this realm, so merry and bright,
The spirit of winter shines pure delight!

Moonlit Migrations

Under the moon, where shadows play,
Reindeer giggle, come what may.
They prance in lines, a silly parade,
Through glimmering snow, their antics displayed.

With twinkling eyes, they dash and dart,
Making snow angels, they fall apart.
They take turns dancing, a silly show,
While snowflakes fall with a gentle flow.

In a magical world of winter's song,
They frolic together, where hearts belong.
With bells a-jingling and laughter loud,
They smear snowflakes on each laughing crowd.

So follow their trail, if you hear a squeal,
Join in their fun — come dance, come feel!
For under the moon, in the shimmering night,
Is laughter galore, oh what a delight!

Midnight Sleigh Rides

At midnight's call, hooves make a sound,
A merry crew of reindeer round.
With jingling bells, they take to flight,
Zooming through stars, what a silly sight!

They race the moon in games of chase,
Dodging snowflakes, oh what a pace!
One tries to dance, another trips,
Laughing, they tumble, doing flips!

A game of tag, they zoom around,
Over the rooftops, they leap and bound.
With noses bright and spirits high,
Jokes in the sleigh as they soar the sky!

Then dripping with snow, they land in glee,
On rooftops waiting for you and me.
They snicker and wink, oh what a crew,
Delivering joy with a laugh or two!

The Guardians of the Evergreen

In the evergreen woods, a sight to behold,
Reindeer prance, oh so bold!
Guardians of laughter, with hearts full of cheer,
They're known for their antics throughout the year!

They play hide and seek among the trees,
Bouncing and leaping, like leaves in the breeze.
One hides beneath a pile of pine,
While others munch on treats so fine!

A riddle is tossed, with giggles galore,
'What's big and furry and loves to explore?'
With winks exchanged and laughter loud,
Any chance to jest, they're so very proud!

The sun sets low, painting skies bright,
As reindeer twirl in the fading light.
With a wink and a nod, they say goodnight,
Guarding the woods till morning light!

Echoes of the Arctic Trail

Across the icy fields, frolicsome they prance,
With winter's whisper, they take a chance.
Sliding on ice, they joke and tease,
One tripped on frost, landing with ease!

Through snow-fluffed valleys, echoes they bring,
Of snorts and snickers, a merry fling!
Bounding like ninjas through blizzards so bright,
They're testing their might, oh what a sight!

In frosty air, they spin and twirl,
Their laughter echoes, helping frost to swirl.
'You missed the snowball!' someone would shout,
Then a barrage of laughter, wrapped up in clout!

As stars blanket skies, their frolics resume,
They light up the night, dispelling the gloom.
With each merry leap, they dance in delight,
Echoes of joy fill the Arctic night!

Stories Carried on the Wind

Under a twilight sky, the stories arise,
Reindeer share legends, beneath the stars' guise.
Of snowstorms and sleigh rides, of laughter and fun,
Whispers of mischief, the tales weigh a ton!

One grins and recalls the time it was told,
How he borrowed the sleigh, and it turned too bold.
With giggles galore, he sped down the lane,
Leaving behind only chuckles and rain!

As tales spin forth, the moon whispers fine,
With antlers aglow, their laughter aligns.
Mysteries of the night, carried on breezes,
Stories of reindeer bring joy that never ceases!

With twinkling eyes, they bid night adieu,
As the dawn's warm glow starts painting the blue.
Each story a treasure, a giggle, a spin,
In every heart, the laughter will win!

The Playful Spirits of the North

In the snow they frolic and jump,
With a twist and a turn, they create a clump.
Tails wagging high, they dance with glee,
Mixing laughter with snowflakes, wild and free.

They play tag with the stars in a dizzying race,
With hooves on the ground, they spin, oh what a pace!
Each leap is a giggle, each bound a delight,
Reindeer pirouette under the moonlight's bright.

With a hiccuping snort and a joyful prance,
They challenge each other to a snowball dance.
Sleds made of laughter, they gather in a line,
Racing through powder, oh so divine!

At night, they sit down, all huddled in a pack,
Sharing tales of mischief, never looking back.
With giggles and snorts, they settle in tight,
Dreaming of pranks till the morning light.

Journey Through the Velvet White

Through blankets of white, they leap and twirl,
In their winter wonderland, they spin and swirl.
Paws in the snow, they make silly tracks,
Creating a map of their zany hijacks.

They sneak past the trees, eyes twinkling with fun,
Playing hide and seek until the day is done.
A snowstorm approaches, they gather the crew,
With cheeks all a-glow, they craft a snow stew!

In the hush of the night, they conquer the chill,
Sliding on ice, they take a wild thrill.
With a chuckle and cheer, they light up the moon,
Turning quiet nights into a lively tune.

With flurries of laughter and a dash of bold,
Their antics are stories that never grow old.
Through the velvet white, they bring joy around,
With every footstep, pure happiness found.

The Magic of the Winter Sky

Under the swirl of the icy night sky,
The reindeer gather, together they fly.
With a jingle of bells, they take to the air,
Chasing the stars, without a single care.

They hold a grand party atop the cold peaks,
With mischief in heart and laughter in squeaks.
Snowflake confetti falls from up high,
As they dance on the clouds, oh how they can fly!

With a flip and a spin, they brighten the frost,
Portraying a magic that's never quite lost.
At dawn's early light, they settle their fight,
Sharing tales of the night, filled with pure delight.

As the sun peeks over, a new day begins,
With giggles and grins, they nuzzle like twins.
For in every turn under the winter sky,
The magic of fun just refuses to die.

Echoes of Ancient Forests

In forests so deep, where stories are spun,
The reindeer explore, always ready for fun.
Like shadows they prance, through branches so wide,
Spilling forth laughter, their joy can't be denied.

They peek through the ferns, and leap over logs,
Playing with echoes, like mischievous frogs.
Each rustle and roar, igniting their cheer,
In this ancient domain, they have nothing to fear.

With a wink and a nod, they tickle the breeze,
Chasing after whispers, moving with ease.
The laughter resounds, an eternal refrain,
In the echoes that bounce through the branches of grain.

When night softly falls and the stars take their seat,
They gather around, with hoofbeats a-beat.
Sharing their secrets and giggling away,
The echoes of forests, where fun's here to stay.

Tales Told by the Snow

In the chill of winter's glow,
Reindeers play in soft white snow.
They prance and dance on frosty ground,
With jingling bells, they make a sound.

With their games, they tease and twirl,
Witty antics make them whirl.
They leap through drifts like fluffy clouds,
Giggling loud, they draw in crowds.

On a sled they ride with glee,
Taking turns with cups of tea.
They wear scarves and silly hats,
And laugh at how they chase the cats.

They sneak a snack behind the trees,
Nibbling treats with such great ease.
Snowflakes fall while they devise,
To prank the moose in their disguise.

Crystalline Dances of the North

Reindeers don their dancing shoes,
To glide and slide, they cannot lose.
With twirls and spins, they steal the show,
Across the ice, their laughter flows.

They spin around the icy lake,
Leaving trails, a zigzag wake.
A snowball fight breaks out in jest,
Who could have guessed they'd be the best?

With glittering lights strung in trees,
They waltz along in winter's breeze.
Elves join in, a funny sight,
Together they dance into the night.

With cheeks all rosy from the chill,
They celebrate with snowy zeal.
In the shimmer of the moonlit skies,
Their funny games bring joyful sighs.

The Merry Mystery of the North

In the cold, a riddle spun,
Reindeers whisper, 'This is fun!'
With antlers crowned in shining light,
They solve the mystery of the night.

They hide the snacks within the snow,
Playing tricks on all they know.
A scavenger hunt, they let it flow,
With giggles that rise like a frosty show.

They chase their tails in merry haste,
Creating patterns, never waste.
Who will win the snowy race?
Each one hopes to earn first place!

Beneath the stars, secrets they share,
Of silly things beyond compare.
With each tease and playful grin,
The merry dance of fun begins.

Enchantment Amongst the Pines

In a glen where shadows play,
Reindeers laugh throughout the day.
They twirl beneath the towering trees,
While snow cascades upon the breeze.

With each stomp, the snowflakes fall,
They gather 'round to sing and call.
A chorus of giggles fills the air,
As playful reindeers strip and share.

In frosty circles, they spin about,
Creating laughter with every shout.
A reindeer wears a flamingo float,
And rides the snow like a silly boat.

They whisper secrets in the night,
Keeping warmth with pure delight.
With merry hearts and spirits high,
Amongst the pines, the fun won't die!

Secrets of the Frostbitten Forest

In the forest where snowflakes lie,
Reindeer giggle as they fly high.
They tickle each other's snowy nose,
And tell silly tales of Christmas woes.

With antlers tangled in bright string lights,
They dance around till the early nights.
They sip cocoa from icy mugs,
And laugh about their playful shrugs.

They pull sleds with a joyful cheer,
Making snow angels from far and near.
In snowball fights, they leap and bound,
Creating laughter, a festive sound.

Under moonlight, they prance and sway,
Reindeer games make a grand display.
They leave hoofprints in the frosty ground,
Secrets of fun in each twist and round.

Legends of the Frosted Path

Tales are spun on frosted trails,
Of snowy hooves and playful gales.
Reindeer race through blizzard's haze,
Inventing more than just a phase.

They claim they're fast, oh yes, the best,
But trip on ice in their jolly jest.
With laughter rolling like fluffy snow,
They stumble and tumble, put on a show.

One finds a hat that's just too big,
Wears it like a crown for a dance and gig.
Another tries to sing a tune,
Turns it into a wintry swoon!

They swap their antlers for a while,
And wear each other's silly style.
Legends built on silly dreams,
Frosted paths hold joyful gleams.

Over the Caves of Ice

Underneath the shimmering sky,
Reindeer peek where the ice caves lie.
They play hide and seek in chilly nooks,
Scaling walls like daring crooks.

In tunnels where the echoes ring,
They laugh and shout, and they all sing.
With frozen bubbles that glimmer bright,
They chase them down through day and night.

One tells tales of crackling ice,
Of slippery slides and haphazard dice.
They giggle as they swoosh and glide,
Riding the waves of a frosty slide.

Through icy paths they leap and bound,
Silly adventures, joy unbound.
Over caves where the frost winds freeze,
Reindeer frolic with such playful ease.

The Heartbeat of the Frozen Tundra

In the tundra, where it's icy clear,
Reindeer gather, spreading cheer.
They tell of a dance that shakes the ground,
Setting off giggles all around.

With every stomp, a thump, a beat,
They make the cold seem warm and sweet.
Their shadows flicker like jolly sprites,
As they choreography goofy flights.

One spins 'round with a jolly grin,
Another cracks up with a silly spin.
They leap through snowdrifts with frost-covered fun,
The heartbeat of joy for everyone.

In the frozen breath of a winter's eve,
Laughter echoes, they hardly believe.
Tundra tales filled with merry sounds,
Reindeer hearts know where joy abounds.

The Evening Parade of the Antlers

In the twilight's soft embrace,
Reindeers strut with lots of grace.
They dance and twirl, a merry sight,
With antlers shining, oh so bright.

They wear the snowflakes like a crown,
Laughing as they prance around.
Each leap a burst of frosty glee,
Echoes through the wintry spree.

The snowy fields become their stage,
As hey-ho, they turn the page.
A comedy in every leap,
And giggles rise from woodland deep.

At dusk, they gather, hearts a-flutter,
To share their tales with sounds of splutter.
With every stomp, their voices cheer,
In the evening parade, full of good cheer.

The Keeper of Winter's Secrets

Sitting high upon a hill,
The keeper grins, he's quite the thrill.
With twinkling eyes and twirling grace,
He knows each reindeer's favorite place.

He winks and nods, the secrets shared,
Of snowy paths and laughs declared.
They giggle wildly, plotting schemes,
As reindeer whisper winter dreams.

With flurries flying all around,
The keeper dances on the ground.
He juggles snowballs, one, two, three,
What a frozen jubilee!

The frosty air, it sparkles bright,
In every heart, he ignites light.
The keeper's tales are full of cheer,
As laughter echoes far and near.

Nature's Velvet Antlers

Soft as clouds, the antlers gleam,
Nature's velvet, like a dream.
They bump and bash through frosty air,
With giggles shared, without a care.

In the snowy fields, they play tag,
Wobbling like a jolly rag.
With playful hops, they dance around,
In their winter frolics, joy is found.

Each tree a friend, each snowflake laughs,
The reindeer share their silly crafts.
Building snowmen, making a cheer,
Nature's plush antlers spreading good cheer.

With every step through winter's woe,
They twirl and leap, a merry show.
Embracing the chill with hearts so warm,
Nature's velvet, oh what a charm!

Rhapsody of the Winter Woods

Deep in the woods, where whispers dwell,
The reindeers hold a playful spell.
With loony leaps and playful spins,
They sing of joy; that's where it begins.

Their antlers jingle, a cheeky sound,
As they chase snowflakes dancing around.
In the moonlight, they frolic free,
In a winter waltz of pure glee.

Chasing shadows, they race and glide,
Through snowy paths, in laughter they ride.
With every jump, they call out loud,
Creating chaos, oh how they proud!

The rhapsody echoes, filling the night,
With every giggle, a pure delight.
In the winter woods, joy abounds,
As reindeers' laughter is all around.

Hoofed Histories at Dusk

As twilight falls and shadows blend,
Hoofed heroes gather, laughter to send.
They swap tales of reindeer games,
With mischief and giggles, never the same.

One boasts of a sprint that left him fleet,
While another claims he danced on his feet.
Caught in a snowbank, they roll and spin,
In the frosty air, their laughter doth win.

Lost in a drift, they'd frolic and play,
Making snow angels at the end of the day.
With antlers adorned in twinkling lights,
They dazzle the moon with their silly sights.

As dusk settles down, the fun will not cease,
For these merry reindeer know laughter's sweet peace.
They prance through the night, a whimsical crew,
And under the stars, their shenanigans brew.

Snowbound Spirits and Starlit Dreams

Under the stars, in blankets of white,
Reindeer giggle, saying, "Oh, what a night!"
With sparkling hoofs, they leap and glide,
Chasing their shadows with joyful pride.

One twirls around like a ballerina,
While another brags of his speed, a true hyena.
They nibble on carrots, the treat of the hour,
Then slide down the hills, their favorite power.

With snowflakes tickling their twinkling muzzles,
They dream of adventures, avoiding the puzzles.
In starlit dreams where the wild things roam,
They build snowy castles, their glimmering home.

And when morning breaks, with silliness clear,
They gather again, full of festive cheer.
No serious talk, just games and delight,
These snowbound spirits, under moonlight.

Trails Through the Silent Snow

On trails made soft by a silvery sheet,
Reindeer trot lightly, skipping with beat.
With ears perked up and eyes full of glee,
They march through the snow, a comical spree.

Catching some snowflakes, they try to munch,
But end up with icicles, stuck in a hunch.
They race each other, with a laugh and a cheer,
Turning snowy paths into playgrounds, oh dear!

A snowball flies straight, too sly to evade,
They tumble and roll in this frosty parade.
With snorts and full grins, they kick up the snow,
Creating a mess, as their antics do flow.

And as the sun sets on their snowy trails,
To the rhythm of joy, every laughter prevails.
With frosty tips tapping like jingle bells,
In the silent snow, their frolic compels.

The Tapestry of Frost and Flight

In a frosty tapestry woven with cheer,
Reindeer spin stories, far and near.
They soar through the night on whimsical wings,
Drafting up mischief that laughter brings.

One's on a mission, delivering giggles,
While another takes off, and in circles, he wiggles.
They play hide and seek in the fuzzy frost,
No one knows where the time has been lost.

Waltzing on rooftops in a snowy ballet,
With each twinkling star, they invent a new play.
They challenge the wind, with skips and with hops,
As icicles dangle, and snow-muffin tops.

So when you look up at the night sky so deep,
Remember the reindeer, their laughter to keep.
With tails all a-wagging and spirits so bright,
They're crafting a legend in the frost and flight.

The Path of the Gentle Giants

In the frosty air, they prance with glee,
Shuffling in shadows, so spry and free.
With jingle bells ringing, they dance through night,
Hooves tapping rhythm, what a silly sight!

They munch on the grass, with a grin so wide,
Wobbling along, in their comical stride.
With antlers held high, they play a grand game,
Pretending to be reindeer, oh, what a claim!

In search of good snacks, they hide with delight,
Stealing the cookies left out overnight.
Bouncing and bounding, they leap and they sway,
Silly giants of night, oh, how they play!

When morning breaks in, they vanish like mist,
Leaving behind just a wink and a twist.
With laughter and cheer, they'll be back again,
The gentle giants, our merry, dear friends!

Frosty Hoofprints in the Moonlight

Under the stars, they skitter and slide,
Frosty hoofprints left winter's cool tide.
Galloping wildly, their joy knows no bounds,
In moonlit meadows, their laughter resounds!

They tumble and trip through soft, snowy flakes,
Chasing their shadows, oh, what silly mistakes!
With snowballs a-flying, they giggle and cheer,
In this frosty playground, there's nothing to fear!

A waltz in the snow, on their delicate hooves,
Their playful antics prove winter improves.
Grinning at strangers, they show off their style,
Warming the hearts with each frosty smile.

As dawn starts to break, they'll rush out of sight,
Dreaming of prancing through next starry night.
Those frosty hoofprints will soon fade away,
Yet memories linger where the antlers play!

A Symphony of Snow and Antlers

In a grand concert under the silver moon,
Reindeer create their own merry tune.
With jingling collars that spark joy and cheer,
A symphony sweet, drawing all to appear!

They gather in circles, and dance with flair,
Rhythm in their hooves, twirling through the air.
Playing hide and seek in the snowy white glow,
These clumsy musicians put on quite a show!

A maestro with antlers leads their grand jam,
While others just bumble, oh, bless their mad plan!
Shooting through drifts, in a flurry of fun,
Their laughter rings out, 'til the night is done.

As notes start to fade with the light of the dawn,
The reindeer will chuckle and stretch with a yawn.
But tomorrow will come, as it surely must do,
To play their next symphony, just for you!

Beneath the Burden of Stars

Under a blanket of shimmering light,
Reindeer look up, oh, what a delight!
With eyes wide as saucers, they gaze at the sky,
Wondering just how those stars got up high!

They tiptoe around in the soft, glistening snow,
Wearing their antlers as crowns, don't you know?
With twinkling arrangements, they strut and they weave,
Creating a dance, as if they believe!

Pretends to be wise with a sage's old grin,
Declaring profound thoughts, like how stars can spin.
Then tripping on snowdrifts, they howl with laughter,
Wonders of night hold their performer's chapter!

As first light appears, they scamper away,
For another wild night, another big play.
Beneath stars so bright, these silly pals thrive,
In the canvas of night, oh, they are alive!

Legends of the Snowy Wilderness

In the snowy woods they prance,
With antlers grand, they love to dance.
They pull the sleighs on Christmas Eve,
And giggle at the tricks they weave.

They race the fox, they chase their tails,
Through fields of white with frosty trails.
With every leap, they share a laugh,
A comedy of hoofed half-drafts.

The moonlight glimmers, spirits high,
As they attempt their comedy fly.
With every clumsy twist and turn,
They make the frozen world adjourn.

A legend born in snow and fun,
For every reindeer, there's a pun.
In snowy nights, they play with glee,
Oh, the joy in wild jubilee!

Frosted Fantasies on Four Legs

Upon the snowy hills they glide,
With jolly thoughts, they must abide.
They dream of peppermint and cheer,
While planning mischief far and near.

In frosted forests, laughter rings,
They twirl and leap on hidden springs.
A snowball fight, oh what a sight,
They scurry fast, their hearts alight.

Their noses twitch, ideas brew,
They plot delights the whole night through.
A game of tag beneath the stars,
They dodge the trees and chase their cars.

In frozen wonder, joy takes flight,
As frosted fantasies ignite.
With every dash, a giggle's shared,
In snowy tales, none are spared!

Celestial Treks Across the Tundra

They trot beneath the twinkling sky,
With starlit paths that never lie.
On cosmic quests through frosty air,
They scheme and dream with joyful flair.

With bounding hops and graceful spins,
They chase the moon, the laugh begins.
A comet's tail, they want to catch,
And make their friends all rise and hatch.

Their antlers sparkle, glitter bright,
As they embark on wondrous flight.
In snowy realms, they share their tales,
Of cosmic trips and silly trails.

With laughter echoing through the night,
Their frosted dreams take wondrous flight.
Each beaming star, a nudge to say,
"Let's frolic more, come join the play!"

Tracks Through the Midnight Wood

In midnight woods, they leave their trace,
With silly stamps, they race and chase.
They whisper jokes to trees around,
In secret tales, good fun is found.

Their hooves create a rhythmic beat,
A joyful dance, a frosty feat.
Each shadow hides a playful glare,
As twinkling eyes gleefully stare.

They weave through branches, skip and jump,
In playful chaos, they make a thump.
A hidden stash of shiny treats,
To share with friends and nibble sweets.

And when the morning light does beam,
They gather 'round and start to dream.
In woodlands vast, they play and play,
With laughter bright, they greet the day!

Woodland Songs and Winter Tales

In the forest, they prance with glee,
Telling jokes with every leap and spree.
Carrots in hand, they laugh and cheer,
Making friends with squirrels, oh so dear.

Around the trees, they play a game,
Trying to catch the falling snowflakes' fame.
Whispers shared in the chilly night,
Planning mischief till morning light.

They draft up plans with a cheeky grin,
To sled down hills and let the fun begin.
With twirls and spins, they glide with flair,
Crashing into snowdrifts, without care!

As moonlight bathes the land in white,
They frolic till dawn, a jovial sight.
In the woodland, laughter fills the air,
A holiday party with naught a care.

Frosty Whispers of the Arctic

In the frosty land, a giggle is heard,
As the reindeer dance, they fly like a bird.
Chasing their tails, a comical scene,
They tumble and roll, all shiny and keen.

With snowball fights, they bring the cheer,
Poking their noses, they conquer with fear.
Sliding on ice, they create a mess,
In their built igloos, they find happiness.

Stories are spun of gigantic snowmen,
Their noses made of carrots, oh what a plan!
They sing to the stars, so bright and bold,
Of adventures and laughter, tales to be told.

As dawn breaks in hues of pink and gold,
They share their secrets, never to withhold.
Frosty whispers, all filled with delight,
Celebrating their antics under the moonlight.

Guardians of the Frozen Realm

In the frozen realm, they keep watchful eyes,
Playing hide and seek beneath icy skies.
With each gentle pounce, they burst into glee,
Chasing their shadows, wild and free.

Dressed in white coats, they blend with the snow,
Hiding from friends, putting on quite a show.
They teach the snowflakes how to twirl,
Like ballerinas, giving winter a whirl.

Crafting snow angels, they laugh and they sing,
While trees dressed in frost, sway with the fling.
Taking breaks for snacks, they munch and crunch,
On frosted carrots, they have a quick lunch.

As night falls softly, they gather around,
Sharing the stories of mischief they found.
Guardians of winter, in laughter, they dwell,
In the icy night air, they cast their spell.

The Dance of the Winter Shadows

As twilight falls, they come out to play,
Dancing in shadows, a whimsical ballet.
With hops and skips, they twist in delight,
painting the ground with laughter so bright.

They twirl with joy, as the stars wink above,
Spinning like tops, in this festive glove.
A raccoon joins in, stealing the scene,
Making the night a madcap routine.

From the trees overhead, the owls observe,
Chortling along, in a feathered curve.
As stories unfold in the cold, crisp air,
These reindeer create, friendships beyond compare.

With the moon as their spotlight, they frolic and glide,
In the dance of shadows, they take great pride.
Embodying fun, every night is their stage,
In this wintery wonderland, they laugh and engage.

Echoes of the Evergreen Spires

In the woods where the tall pines sing,
Reindeer dance, it's a cheerful thing.
With antlers high, they prance around,
Making merry, no troubles found.

They play tag with the trees all day,
In a world that's just a snowy play.
Sledding down hills, they giggle with glee,
Spreading joy, so wild and free.

With bells that jingle and a wink of an eye,
They plot silly antics 'neath the wide, blue sky.
Like clowns at a circus, they steal the show,
Reindeer games in the frosty glow.

At night they gather, share tales of the day,
Making hot cocoa with marshmallows to play.
'Tis a laugh riot, these creatures so spry,
Echoes of merriment fill the night sky.

Celestial Navigators of the North

Stargazing reindeer wearing shades,
Map their routes through snowy glades.
With a compass made of candy canes,
They giggle at their navigational gains.

One's a pilot, one's a co-pilot too,
In an imaginary sleigh that flew.
They chart courses to cookie land,
With edible maps drawn by hand.

In this crew of celestial delight,
They have a giggle on a starry night.
Pointing out constellations made of cheese,
They snack and laugh in the frosty breeze.

With sleigh bells ringing, they take their flight,
Like comets brightening the chilly night.
Navigators of the skies, with flair,
Bringing joy to the midnight air.

Fables of Frost and Flight

Reindeer tales of winter fun,
Fables told under the warming sun.
With frostbit hooves, they stomp around,
Bouncing like bunnies on snowy ground.

They've got the moves of a dance routine,
Strutting in sync, like a merry scene.
With a twist and a turn, they leap with grace,
Who knew frosty frolics held such a pace?

Lobbing snowballs, their laughter rings,
Creating chaos, the joy it brings!
Once a snowman got up for the show,
And joined their antics to steal the glow.

At the end of the day, when shadows grow,
They tell stories wrapped in a snowy glow.
With each chilly tale, hearts warm and bright,
Frosty fables that tickle the night.

Beneath the Silver Moon

Beneath a moon that shines so bright,
The reindeer frolic, a comical sight.
With a hop and a skip, they jump in delight,
Hoping to catch a glowing firefly light.

They swap their tales of the day gone by,
With playful nudges and laughter nearby.
Under twinkling stars, they choose to tease,
Tickling each other with frosty pine leaves.

One reindeer claims he can fly like a bird,
But trips on his antlers, oh how absurd!
Their chuckles echo through the woodland hall,
As they share this memory, pure joy for all.

In the glow of the night, with friends ever near,
The merriment dances like frost in the air.
A moonlit gathering, where laughter's the tune,
As the reindeers play, beneath the silver moon.

Heritage of the Hooved

In the woods, they play and prance,
With antlers high, they take a chance.
Nibbling on the berries so sweet,
Wearing snow like a fancy sheet.

They dance around in sleighs galore,
Telling tales of days of yore.
With little bells that tinkle bright,
They frolic in the soft moonlight.

The snowflakes tickle as they run,
Hiding secrets, oh what fun!
Each jump leads to a playful chase,
A parade of joy, a friendly race.

With stories spun of frost and cheer,
They craft their magic, year by year.
And as they bound through trees so thick,
They craft the world's most jolly trick.

The Map of Winter's Heart

Mapping out a snowy spree,
With a giggle for company.
They follow paths where snowflakes twirl,
Unraveling dreams in a swirling whirl.

Their hoofprints dance in wavy lines,
Leading to the land of pine.
With joy, they test the icebound trails,
Sharing laughs like chiming bells.

A treasure hunt with treats galore,
Candy canes and something more.
They sip from streams of chocolate flow,
In the forest, they steal the show.

So if you wander through the frost,
Look for where the giggles are tossed.
For in this map of winter's art,
Lies every reindeer's winking heart.

Beneath the Shimmering Stars

Underneath the twinkling lights,
They giggle and spin with delight.
Reindeer games in the midnight air,
Snowball fights without a care.

Flipping over, they bump and slide,
On icy hills, they take a ride.
Rolling snowballs, not too tall,
Until they tumble with a giggly fall.

Whispers echo in the night sky,
"Wish on a star!" the little ones cry.
With playful nudges, they tease each other,
The best of friends, like sister and brother.

So dance beneath those sparkle beams,
In winter's cold, they spin their dreams.
A reindeer's chuckle is quite the sound,
As laughter lifts and swirls around.

The Reindeer's Secret Paths

Through hidden trails where no one goes,
They find delight in flurries of snow.
With playful hops and little kicks,
They dodge the branches, play funny tricks.

A secret glade with treats in store,
Candy frosting, oh, and more!
They twirl and leap with snowflakes bright,
Every turn brings pure delight.

Behind the trees, they pull a stunt,
A leapfrog game! It's quite the hunt.
With every hop, a burst of cheer,
Their laughter ringing loud and clear.

In the night, they paint the snow,
With hoofprints showing where to go.
The paths they carve, oh what a sight,
In a world of giggles, pure delight.

Dance of the Arctic Shadows

In the snowy glens where they prance,
Reindeers in hats put on a dance.
With antlers adorned in tinsel bright,
They twirl and spin under the moonlight.

Cups of cocoa spill when they glide,
Sledding down hills, they take in stride.
Chasing snowflakes, laughing with glee,
Oh, what a sight, come dance with me!

The penguins clap from their icy perch,
While seals join in with a lively lurch.
They stomp their hooves, shake their tails,
Creating stories of fun-filled trails.

So grab your boots, come join in cheer,
With reindeers and friends, let's spread good cheer!
In the Arctic shadows, a giggle's found,
Where joy and laughter know no bounds.

Echoes in the Winter Woods

In winter woods, where the pine trees sway,
Reindeer giggle, adding to the play.
With each leap and bound, they cavort and weave,
Echoes of laughter dance on the eve.

They make a snowman with a carrot nose,
And tie a red scarf around his toes.
Then do the cha-cha on frosty ground,
Making footprints that spiral around.

One wears a wig made of fluffy white,
While another dons sunglasses, a silly sight.
They pose for a selfie with snowflakes in flight,
As echoes of joy cut through the night.

The owls awake to this raucous scene,
Chiming in with a hoot, rather keen.
In the winter woods, it's a merry hum,
With reindeer antics, oh how they come!

A Reindeer's Tale

Gather 'round for a tale to share,
Of reindeer antics beyond compare.
With a wink and a nod, they plot and scheme,
Life in the snow is one big dream.

They traded their bells for jingle hats,
And played tug-of-war with the forest rats.
Zooming through trees with a giggly shriek,
Who knew reindeer could be so cheek?

One decided to bake a big cake,
But forgot to add in the flour, for Pete's sake!
With sprinkles on hooves, it ended a mess,
But laughter erupted, nothing less.

So raise your cups and toast to this crew,
With sweet tales of snow and the silly things too.
A reindeer's life, a joyous trail,
Filled with laughter, it's a grand tale.

The Call of the Snowy Wild

In the call of the wild where the frostbite bites,
Reindeer gather to share their delights.
A karaoke night 'neath the shimmering stars,
They belt out tunes underneath Mars.

With voices like bells, off-key and bold,
They sing of the winters and stories retold.
While squirrels dance, and the critters cheer,
Oh, the snowy wild, a party so near!

One tries to rap, but slips on the ice,
His rhymes tangled up, oh, isn't it nice?
Laughter erupts from the snowy throng,
As they croon about cheese—it won't take long!

From the snowy peaks to valleys below,
Reindeer know just how to steal the show.
In the call of the wild, with cheer in their hearts,
They bring us together, that's where fun starts.

Milton Keynes UK
Ingram Content Group UK Ltd.
UKHW021928011224
451790UK00005B/65